LIFE SKILLS
IN THE PACIFIC

Tourism

Richard Jones & Jennifer Miller

OXFORD

OXFORD
UNIVERSITY PRESS

Oxford University Press is a department of the University of Oxford. It furthers the University's objective of excellence in research, scholarship, and education by publishing worldwide. Oxford is a registered trademark of Oxford University Press in the UK and in certain other countries.

Published in Australia by
Oxford University Press
253 Normanby Road, South Melbourne, Victoria 3205, Australia

First published 2011

ISBN 978 0 19 557599 6

Typeset by Polar Design Pty Ltd
Illustrated by Mairi Feeger
Printed in China by Golden Cup Printing Co. Ltd

Contents

Foreword

Tourists visit Papua New Guinea for many different reasons – pleasure, adventure, relaxation and culture. Small-scale village-based tourism projects are popular with tourists. These projects can improve the quality of life for local people and provide a small income. Running a successful tourism project is a challenge but communities can learn lessons from other people's successes and achievements.

This book aims to provide a basic introduction to the practical life skills of running a small, community-based tourism project in Papua New Guinea.

Acknowledgments

We would like to thank the many dedicated teachers and community workers who teach students about practical life skills, tourism and how to make a living. We also dedicate this book to the Papua New Guinean entrepreneurs and communities who have run successful community-based tourism businesses and who have welcomed us into their community and culture. Many of their stories and lessons are in this book.

Jennifer Miller & Richard Jones

Notes for teachers

This textbook is written for primary and secondary students and their teachers.

The knowledge, skills and attitudes in the text develop these learning outcomes from the Making a Living, Business Studies and Tourism Studies syllabuses in Papua New Guinea.

Making a Living Grades 6, 7 and 8

6.3.3 Participate in projects to meet identified needs and opportunities for improvement within the school

7.3.3 Initiate and plan cooperative projects that encourage community and school participation

8.3.3 Plan and undertake an enterprising project to enable them to make a living

Business Studies Grades 9 and 10

9.4.1 Design and write a small business enterprise plan

9.4.2 Implement and manage a small business enterprise applying ethical business practices

10.2.1 Develop a small business plan individually or in teams

10.2.2 Run a small business enterprise applying ethical business practices

10.2.3 Evaluate the business project to determine its viability

Option 4 The Business of Tourism

a) Identify and describe the needs and wants of tourists as consumers

b) Identify and describe key tourist markets

c) Demonstrate an understanding of tourism promotion and marketing techniques

Tourism Studies Grades 11 and 12

1 Demonstrate an understanding of tourism at the local, national, regional and international level

2 Describe and explain the growth of local, national, regional and global tourism

3 Identify the role of tourism in the economic growth of a country

4 Demonstrate an understanding of the impact of tourism at individual, local, national, regional and global levels

5 Demonstrate an understanding of the principles of good management and customer service

6 Communicate tourism information in a variety of ways and settings

There are many activities in the text for the students to complete and discuss. These can be used for self study or as teaching and learning activities in class. They are designed for maximum student participation and developing life skills.

Introduction

Making a living through **community-based tourism** is challenging and interesting. Many communities in Papua New Guinea have run successful tourism projects. These help provide a small income to the families and communities.

This book aims to share some of the skills, knowledge and important lessons about how to set up, run and make a small income from your tourism project.

Why do people come and visit our country?

A tourist is a person who travels from their home place to visit another place for pleasure.

International tourists come to visit your country for many reasons:

- for adventure
- for relaxation
- to experience a different culture
- to see unique wildlife and plants
- to buy crafts
- to contribute to development
- to learn about history.

Some international tourists will spend their time in large hotels and resorts or on special tours. However, some tourists will want to meet local people, learn about the culture and see how they live. They can do this by staying in a village or walking in the bush. This is community-based tourism.

There are also an increasing number of **local tourists**. These are people – usually from the cities – who travel to another part of their own country. They are looking for an interesting experience, or maybe to see friends and family.

Chapter 1 Why would tourists visit our community?

Think about what your community has to offer. Papua New Guinea has unique cultures and a beautiful, untouched environment. People keep alive the rich traditions of their ancestors. There are white sand beaches, coral reefs, huge mountains, volcanoes, and rainforests. The birds, animals, fish and plant life are world famous.

Many **tourists** will want to visit your country.

Activity 1.1 What does our community have to offer tourists?

Brainstorm what is special about your community under these headings. What does your community have that makes it interesting and unique?

Case study: Attracting tourists through culture

A remote community in the cool mountains of Papua New Guinea was interested in tourism. This group of villages is only accessible by light aircraft.

Local people knew they had a unique culture, especially their traditional houses and cultural celebrations and headdresses. They wanted to share these with tourists.

First of all, the community built a bush material guesthouse and a beautiful garden with views across the valley and mountains. They knew that a lot of tourists visited the closest town, so they advertised their guesthouse in the hotels and resorts in that town.

The guesthouse offered bushwalking tours from the guesthouse to the next airstrip, through the forest and mountains.

Realising that the Independence Day holiday was a popular time for tourists, they advertised a regular cultural festival with traditional dances and demonstrations of local crafts. This now attracts small but interested groups of international tourists and is a regular feature of the tourism calendar in the province.

What did this community have to offer?

1. What was special about this community?
2. Why do you think international tourists were interested in visiting them?
3. What did the local people do to attract tourists?
4. What is the most important lesson from their tourism projects?

Every community has something that could interest tourists. However, to be successful in making a living from tourism you will need to plan and carry out your project carefully.

The steps to a successful community-based tourism project are described in Chapter 4.

It is also a good idea to think about why visitors might not want to visit your community. If you know what might stop people from coming you can plan better. Some reasons that might stop people from coming to your community include:

Poor security

Poor sanitation, food and water

Dishonesty or cheating

Lazy or uninformed guides

Poor advertising

Damage to your environment or culture

Chapter 2 The impact of tourism

Many tourists just visit large resorts. Some of these are owned by international companies. However, there are many smaller tourism businesses which are locally owned. At the village level, there are small family-run or community-run tourism projects.

Each kind of tourism has an impact on the community and its people.

Resorts and hotels

Positive impacts

- They employ many local people who earn a regular wage and learn useful skills.
- They often work with community-based projects.
- They are able to advertise overseas to attract people to the country.
- They can offer expensive activities like diving.

Negative impacts

- The profits usually go to the owners or overseas.
- There is a large impact on local environment (sewerage, water supply).
- They can keep tourists from experiencing village life and culture.
- They might exploit local people, environment and cultures.

Impact of large resorts and hotels

1. Are there any large resorts or hotels in your province? List them.
2. Who owns them?
3. What are the positive and negative impacts of these resorts and hotels?
4. Do you know anyone who has worked in a large resort or hotel? What were their experiences?

Community-based tourism

Positive impacts

- The profits stay in the community.
- Tourists get to see the real country, learn about people's lives and experience traditional culture.
- It promotes self-reliance and local economic development.
- Community-based tourism is more sustainable.

Negative impacts

- Visitors can be irregular, so it is not a reliable income source.
- It can lead to jealousy and conflict in the community.
- It can be hard to advertise to international tourists.
- It can disrupt day-to-day life for people in the village.
- Visitors can have an impact on culture and the environment.

Impact of community-based tourism

1. Are there any community-based tourism projects in your province? Label these on a map.
2. Who owns them?
3. What are the positive and negative impacts of these projects?
4. How many visitors do they get a year?
5. Do you know anyone who has worked in a community-based tourism project? What were their experiences?

Like any kind of business, tourism will have an impact in the community. It is usually more **sustainable** than other kinds of development such as mining, logging and industrial fishing. This means that the resources will stay in the community and will not be overused or damaged.

Tourists will not take anything apart from photographs and bought crafts and artefacts. They will usually not damage or destroy what they have come to see, such as your forests, birds or reefs. However, any income generation project will have an impact in your community.

It is important to plan ahead and think about these impacts before starting your project.

Chapter 3 Community-based tourism activities

Your tourism activities will depend on what makes your community interesting and different. In Activity 1.1 you brainstormed what makes your community attractive to visitors.

Some of the different types of tourism activities are listed below.

Community guesthouse and village stays

Staying in a community guesthouse, usually made out of traditional materials, is a popular activity. Tourists like to experience village life. The guesthouse can also be used for local gatherings and meetings when tourists are not staying there. You can read more about the dos and don'ts of running a community guesthouse in Chapter 5.

Tours to places of interest

Tours are a simple way of earning a small income. Tours could be to waterfalls, wrecks, caves, viewpoints, places where birds display, or simple beautiful walks.

Often there is a traditional, environmental or historical reason for the tour and the tour guide will need to be able to explain and talk about the tour. They will also need permission to visit those areas. You can read more about running tours in Chapter 6.

Bushwalking, hiking and mountain climbing

These are longer adventure walks of a day or more. The guide would need to be fit and strong. They would need to know the trail well and know what to do in an emergency.

Organising food, water, shelter and porters is usually the job of the guide.

Popular trails in Papua New Guinea include the Mount Wilhelm summit, Kokoda Track and Black Cat Trail. You can read more in Chapter 7.

Fishing, canoeing and snorkelling

The waters around the Pacific are rich with reefs and fish. Many tourists like to swim, snorkel and fish.

Safety and getting permission are both important. You might also need equipment like a canoe or boat, fishing lines, snorkels and diving masks.

Inland rivers, waterfalls and lakes can also be places for swimming and fishing.

Surfing

Surfing is popular with adventure tourists. The surf seasons for PNG are:

- **June–September:** southern coasts
- **October–April:** northern coasts like Vanimo, Madang and Kavieng.

Running a surf community business needs a guesthouse and good **surf breaks** nearby. International tourists usually bring their own surfboards.

Arts and crafts

Making and selling traditional arts, crafts and objects is a popular tourist business but it can be competitive.

Usually you will sell during a craft market or festival or to a hotel or resort. You will need to decide your prices and whether you want to negotiate with the tourists.

Arts and crafts can include pottery, weaving, baskets, carvings, shell money and traditional jewellery. Chapter 8 is about arts and crafts.

Cultural events

Cultural events can attract tourists from all over the world. Special festivals such as the Goroka Show in Eastern Highlands can attract hundreds of international visitors.

Your community could take part in one of the larger festivals or shows or try to attract people to a smaller, unique community festival.

It is important that local taboos and traditions are respected.

Wildlife and plants

Taking tourists to see special wildlife or plants is a popular kind of tour. For example, birdwatchers travel from all over the world to see the amazing birds of paradise.

Butterflies, rare animals and birds are all popular. Tourists also like to learn about plants used for traditional medicines. They like beautiful flowers and trees.

Make sure you know the names of the birds and insects. Draw a map of where to find them at different times of day.

Do not disturb their habitat by over-hunting and destroying the forest. This will ruin the animals' nests and homes. The tourists will have nothing to see.

Activity 3.1 Advantages and disadvantages

Different community-based tourism activities have advantages and disadvantages.

Choose at least three of the activities above and list what the advantages and disadvantages are. This example is for cultural events.

Advantages of cultural events as a tourist activity in my community	Disadvantages of cultural events as a tourist activity in my community
• Lots of people would benefit • Preserve our traditions	• Hard to organise on time • Need to share money

Chapter 4 Steps to successful tourism

Making a living from tourism is like any other community-based income-generating project. You need to be clear about what you are doing and have the skills, knowledge and attitudes to run the small business successfully.

You will also need the support of your community and a clear understanding of who will do what. Deciding what to do with any money you make is also important.

Self-reliance is crucial to your future and the development of your country. Tourism is one sustainable way of earning some money. You will not become rich, but, if you work hard, you might make a little money to support you and your family.

Being an entrepreneur

An **entrepreneur** is someone who starts and runs their own business.

An entrepreneur:

- has a positive attitude
- is organised
- is hardworking
- is determined
- is able to overcome setbacks
- is a good problem solver
- is able to think about what the tourists and the community want and need
- knows when to ask for help.

Am I an entrepreneur?

1 What personal qualities do you have that would help you to start and run a small income-generating tourism project?

For example:

- able to plan ahead
- can think about a long-term goal
- able to get along with people.

2 What skills, knowledge and attitudes do you think you need to develop to be a better entrepreneur?

3 Who could help you develop these skills and knowledge?

Community-based tourism planning

This section explains the main steps you will need to take to set up and run a successful income-generating business. It is important to complete each step before moving onto the next one. Poor planning will harm your business.

Remember that sometimes you might not be successful at one of the steps. A determined businessperson does not give up. They learn their lessons, develop new skills, and start again.

Key questions to think about at each step

1
Investigating what tourists and your community want
Your idea for a business

- What will attract tourists to your project?
- How will the community benefit?
- What would be positive and negative impacts?
- Who else is doing something similar? Could you work in partnership?
- How many tourists might visit?
- How will they get to your community?
- What skills, resources and information do you need?
- What problems might there be and how would you solve them?

2
Planning and designing
Consulting the community

- How long will each step of the project take?
- Who will work on the project?
- Who do you need to get permission from in the community?
- How much money will you need to start your project? Do you need a bank account?
- How much money will you charge? Is this enough to cover your costs?
- Will you need any training or more information?

3
Marketing and advertising
Making and building

- How will tourists learn about your tourism activity?
- How will tourists contact you or visit your place?
- Do you need any printed materials?
- Who can help you in your area (resorts, hotels, tour operators, tourism office)?
- How will you manage any building or making?

4
Running the tourism project

Making an income, keeping records, etc.

- How will you manage any money?
- Who will look after the tourists?
- Will they need any training?
- How will you keep the records of your business?
- Which community members need to be kept informed?
- How will you solve any problems?

5
Evaluating what you have learnt

- How do you know you have been successful?
- What problems did you have and were your solutions good ones?
- What were the surprises and achievements?
- What was the feedback from the tourists?
- What did the community think?
- How much income did you make? What did you use it for?
- What will you do differently next time? What will you do next in the business?

Developing and running your project will need the support and cooperation of your family and community. It is important that they are involved.

Speaking to family and community leaders and doing some **market research** are good first steps.

Activity 4.2 Market research

Market research is when a business asks its customers what they want or need. You can do this to find out whether tourists are interested in your planned tourism project.

Here are some example questions:

- Which three activities would you be interested in doing in a traditional village?
- How many nights would you like to stay in a traditional village?
- What is the maximum you would pay for these carvings? *(show pictures of three different carvings)*

Design a simple questionnaire to give to international tourists at a nearby resort or hotel about your planned tourist activity. The answers should help you plan.

Activity 4.3 Guest speaker

Meet and interview a guest speaker who has run, or worked with, a small community-based tourism project.

Here are some example questions you could ask:

Why did these work well?

What were the successes?

What did you learn from your market research?
How much money did you spend setting up the project?
How much money did you earn in your first year?
What were the problems and how did you solve them?
How did you keep the tourists safe and secure?
How many tourists visited/bought something?
What is the most important lesson you learnt?

Chapter 5

Running a community guesthouse

Building and running a community guesthouse is a popular way of earning a small income.

Coastal guesthouse

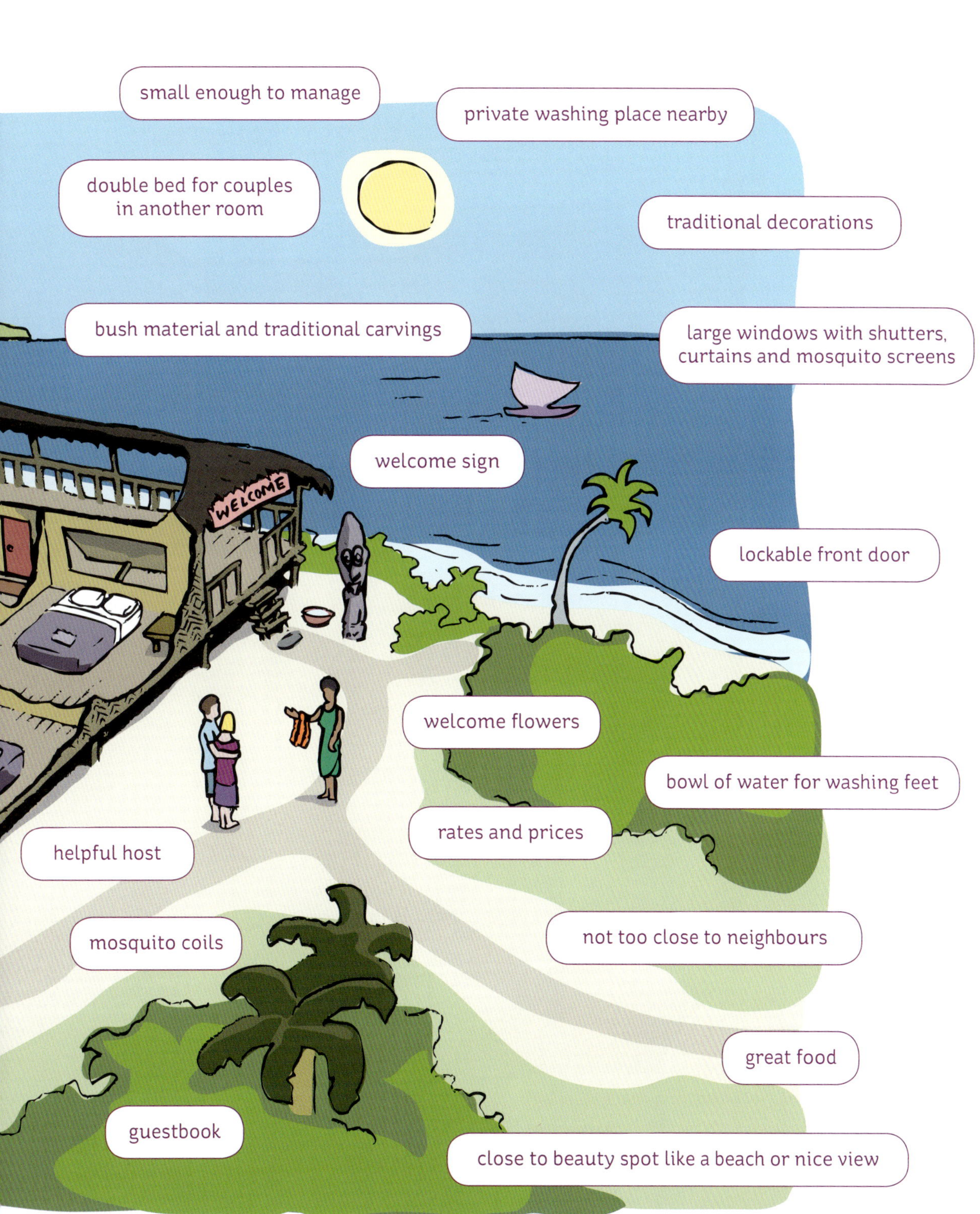
small enough to manage
private washing place nearby
double bed for couples in another room
traditional decorations
bush material and traditional carvings
large windows with shutters, curtains and mosquito screens
welcome sign
WELCOME
lockable front door
welcome flowers
bowl of water for washing feet
rates and prices
helpful host
mosquito coils
not too close to neighbours
great food
guestbook
close to beauty spot like a beach or nice view

Highlands guesthouse

beautiful view over mountains or forest
bush material and traditional carvings
warm
balcony and chairs for relaxing
clean water
windows with shutters, curtains and fly wire
great food
lantern or solar lighting
guestbook
lockable front door
WELCOME
helpful host
welcome flowers
rates and prices
nice gardens and flowers
dry paths

Case study: A successful guesthouse

This guesthouse has been operating successfully for many years. It is located on a beautiful part of coastline several hours' drive away from a town with many hotels and resorts.

What makes this guesthouse so special?

- traditional-style houses on a white sandy beach
- large balconies facing the sea for relaxing
- excellent food with different menus
- clean tank water
- cool river for private bathing
- cleaned daily and well-organised
- private and safe
- knowledgeable and friendly family
- solar power lighting
- easy to contact by mobile phone or through the local tourist office.

Apart from the beautiful and quiet location, its best attraction is excellent surfing and snorkelling.

The most important features

1 Which features of this guesthouse are the most attractive ones to tourists? Sort these features into a top ten list.

2 Why do you think tourists prefer traditional-style houses?

3 Which features of a guesthouse are essential?

4 Where would you build a guesthouse for tourists to your village? Why?

What do tourists want at a village guesthouse?

A traditional and well-built house

Tourists want to feel as if they are living in the village. You should build your guesthouse from traditional materials. If you must have a corrugated iron roof, cover the underside with a woven mat.

Tips

A traditional roof is cooler and more attractive than a corrugated iron roof.

Your house should have:

- a great view and a comfortable place to sit and relax
- clean and aired mattresses with fresh cotton sheets
- single and double beds
- traditional furniture, carvings and decorations
- mosquito nets, fly wire, curtains and wooden shutters
- lanterns, candles or solar lighting
- a locked door.

Tips

- The land where the guesthouse is built will belong to someone, maybe your family or the school. Get written permission before you start building. Explain to them how this will benefit them too.
- It is smarter to build a small two-bedroom guesthouse with a balcony to start with until you find out how many visitors you will be able to get.

Activity

5.2 Design your perfect community guesthouse

1 Draw a map showing its location.

2 Draw a floor plan showing where you will build each room, door, window and balcony.

3 Sketch what the guesthouse will look like from each side.

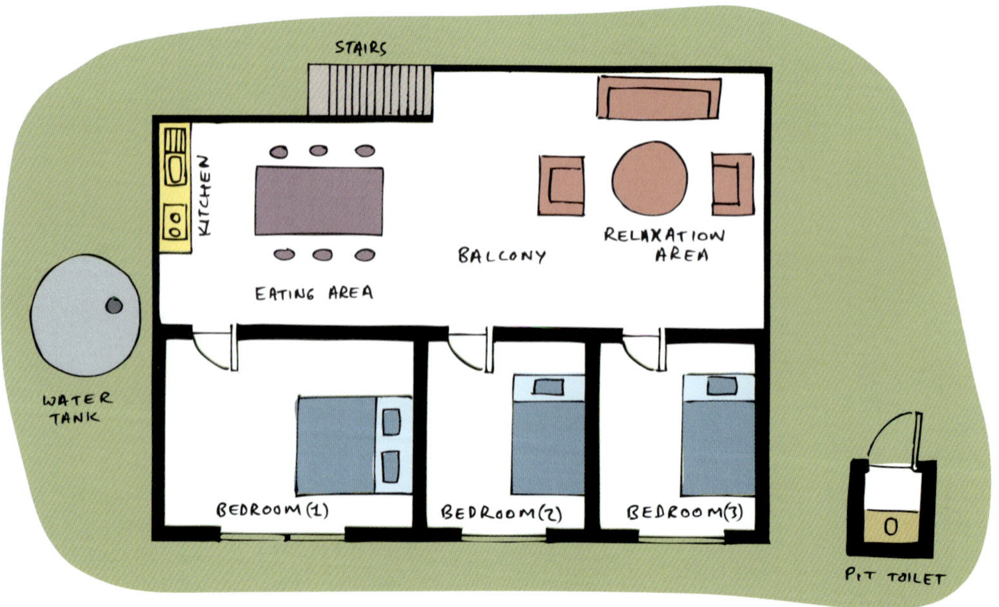

4. List what furniture to make (e.g. one double bed, one hammock, one outside dining table and benches).
5. List what goods you will need to buy (e.g. mosquito net, kerosene lamp, fly wire).
6. Plan the toilet, shower and any other buildings or *haus win* you will need.

Privacy and security

Visitors will want privacy. Curtains, wooden shutters, a secure door and a fence around the guesthouse are all good ideas.

Children in your community will be very interested in your guests, so make sure you establish clear rules for how you want the children to behave.

Clean toilets

Clean toilets are a must for any tourism project. Building a Western toilet is difficult so instead you can build a good ventilated pit latrine (VPL).

- ✓ Stock it with plenty of toilet paper.
- ✓ Clean it daily.
- ✓ Make sure it has a lock.
- ✓ A lid on the toilet seat is a good idea.
- ✓ Place a covered bowl of water and soap by the toilet. Change the water twice a day.
- ✓ The toilet should be in a private and safe place that is not too far from the guesthouse.
- ✓ Build a path to the toilet so it is easy to find at night.

Tips

- Any pit toilet should be built in a safe place where it will not contaminate any water sources.
- Will your family or community also use the toilet? If they will, establish rules to keep it clean and healthy.

Clean water and somewhere private to wash

This is very important. You do not want your guests to get sick. If you do not have a water tank or good well, you should boil all water.

Tourists also like to keep clean. Provide somewhere private for washing.

- ✓ Give tourists a bowl of hot water and soap before meals (don't forget to wash your own hands!).
- ✓ Build a private washing or shower room for bucket showers.
- ✓ Hot water is nice for tourists in the mountains.
- ✓ Have clean towels available.
- ✓ If tourists want their clothes washed, decide if you will charge for this. Often they will wash their own.

Tips

Tourists understand that clean water is limited in villages, especially in the dry season. How will you ensure they do not use too much water?

Great food

You should have a simple menu. Tourists like traditional foods, fruits and vegetables more than processed foods. Food hygiene is very important.

Some tourists like to help work the garden, and collect and make traditional foods like sago and tapioca.

Tips

- Are your guests **vegetarian**? Are there some foods they do not like to eat? When would your guests like to eat? Tourists usually eat their evening meal earlier than local people.
- Who will do the cooking and wash the plates? How will you pay them? How will you get the food from your community?

Design menus for your guests

1 Design a nutritious and interesting menu for your guests for two days and nights. Follow these guidelines:

- Use local foods, meat, eggs and fruits as much as possible.
- Prepare traditional dishes whenever possible.
- Try not to use too many store goods and soft drinks like cordial. Coconut water, fresh juices and tea are healthier.
- Use homemade foods (scones, bread rolls, pancakes) bought from the community.
- Offer breakfast, morning tea, lunch and evening meal.
- Choose foods that are straightforward to prepare.

2 Now calculate the cost and what you would charge (e.g. K10 for breakfast) so you still make a profit.

3 Prepare a neat final copy of your menu.

MENU

Mountain Paradise Guesthouse

K10 Breakfast: pancakes with local honey, local fruits, and locally baked bread scones, tea

K15 Lunch: Omelette made with eggs from our hens, fresh bread or boiled rice, fruits, coconut milk

K20 Dinner: Chicken cooked in coconut milk, taro or sweet potato, local vegetables

Clear prices

Tourists are usually travelling on a budget and they like to know what things will cost. They do not like it if you change prices suddenly. Display your guesthouse rates clearly.

Tips

- It is important to set your prices carefully. What do other nearby guesthouses charge?
- Make sure you keep a receipt book and check that your guests understand the costs. The sign with the prices should be clear and simple to understand.

How much would you charge?

1 Calculate how much money you would need to set up your guesthouse.

2 Work out what the monthly running costs would be (food, toilet rolls, lamp fuel, cleaning materials, etc.).

3 Now decide on your prices. Consider the following questions:

- How many guests are you expecting each year?
- Where can you make money? (Meals and tours are good ways of making extra income, especially if you use home-grown food.)
- How much money do you need for 1) repaying the cost of building the guesthouse, and 2) running costs?

4 Design a welcome sign and price sign for your guesthouse.

Peace and quiet

Many guests will want peace and quiet – a nice balcony with a view, a quiet place to sit and read, and a comfortable bed or hammock. Try not to disturb your visitors if they are relaxing. If they just want to relax, let them. Do not allow loud parties, drunkenness or fights near the guesthouse.

Tips

- Be imaginative in the design of your guesthouse (for example, build it around a tree or over water).
- Keep a guestbook and have homemade business cards to give to guests.
- Welcome guests with tea or coconut milk – first impressions count.

Decide on one person who will be the main **host**. Female tourists might be more comfortable with a woman host. The host can check if there are any problems and share information on tours and activities. They should speak good English if possible and be neat, well-dressed and confident.

Home stays

An alternative to building a whole new guesthouse is to offer a **home stay**. This is when a tourist stays with you in a room in your house.

Some advantages of a home stay are:

- they are cheap to set up
- tourists will see how your family really lives
- it gives tourists a chance to learn your language and culture.

Some disadvantages of a home stay are:

- there is little privacy for you or the tourist
- you have to keep a spare room and bedding for the tourist. Most Pacific houses are crowded with family.
- it disrupts the life of the family.

Research

What do your family members think about a home stay? Write several research questions and then interview members of your family for their views:

- mother
- father
- children
- grandparents
- neighbours.

Are there any differences between the people's opinions? Would your family like to host a home stay tourist?

Chapter 6 Tours and activities

One way of attracting tourists to your guesthouse is to offer **tours** and other activities. Tours can also be organised for tourists staying at other guesthouses or hotels.

A tour is a short trip to a local place of interest. It might take an hour or a whole day.

Local places of interest could include:

- a waterfall or swimming hole
- a historical site such as a World War 2 wreck
- a magnificent view
- a traditional place such as a skull cave
- a pretty beach for snorkelling or swimming.

Tours can include activities such as:

- a rainforest walk
- bird or insect watching
- looking for garden foods or special traditional plants
- lessons on how to cook traditional foods
- watching traditional crafts being made
- a canoe ride or rafting
- a cycle trip
- watching traditional dancing or trying on traditional dress
- a guided walk through a village or gardens.

Which tours could you run in your community?

Brainstorm at least three different tours which you could run in your community. For each tour decide:

- who would be the guide
- how long the tour would last
- who you would need permission from
- whether you would ask for money for that tour.

Large resorts also run tours in which you could make some money by working as a guide. However, there is no reason why a community cannot run its own tours.

Planning a tour

Running a successful tour will need a careful plan.

You will need to think about:

- what you will do before, during and after the tour
- when you will do the tour and how long it will take
- who will be the tour guide
- what they might talk about with the tourists
- whether you need permission to visit a place
- what might go wrong on a tour and what you would do about it
- how much will you charge and who will receive money.

This is an example of a plan for a tour.

TOUR: TRADITIONAL POT MAKING
WHERE: Dorum village
THE GUIDES: Junior Jones and Matilda Moro
CHARGE: K50 per tourist (K15/bus, K20/local potters, K15/guides)

TWO DAYS BEFORE THE TOUR

1. Contact Dorum villagers with details as per our arrangement.
2. Arrange minibus from Zippy Transport as per our agreement. Remind them to send a good driver.

ONE DAY BEFORE THE TOUR

1. Visit the tourists at their guesthouse and confirm pick up and return times and numbers of tourists. Collect money.
2. Call Dorum and confirm numbers of tourists and arrival times.
3. Call Zippy Transport and confirm.
4. Check guide pack (umbrellas, water bottles, charged mobile phone, credit for phone, numbers for Zippy Transport, village and tourists, first aid kit, snacks).

DAY OF THE TOUR:

7.30am	Reminder calls to tourists, Dorum villagers and Zippy Transport.
8.30am	Meet bus. Check it has fuel, good tyres and good driver.
9.00am	Pick up tourists from guesthouse. Give introductory talk about Dorum, guides, safety, cultural rules (e.g. photos and dressing) and return time.
9.15am	Drive to village. Learn guests' names. Answer any questions.
9.40am	Arrive in Dorum. Introduce community leader. Guided tour of village (houses, food gardens, traditional clothes, history, location of male and female toilets).
10.00am	Go to pottery making area. Introduce the potters. Pottery demonstration.
11.00am	Go to village marketplace. Explain prices and that there is no haggling. Show guests beach area and allow them to explore. Payment to potters.
12.00pm	Back on bus. Return to guesthouse. Thank tourists. Give out tour leaflets, your contact information and feedback forms. Payment to bus owners.

Design a tour plan

From your list of possible tours from Activity 6.1, choose one and design a simple plan for running the tour using a similar format to the design above.

For example:

- a traditional food gathering and cooking tour
- a walk to a pretty waterfall
- a visit to a spirit house
- weaving bilums
- a visit to a war memorial.

From your plan you can tell your tourists the **itinerary**. This is a simple set of instructions and description for the tour.

On the next page is an example of an itinerary you would give to a tourist. You should illustrate it with photos or drawings if you can. Then it can be an advertisement for your tour.

Visit a traditional coastal village surrounded by thick jungle and rich gardens where generations of local potters have created the unique Dorum Pottery for trade, decoration and use. There will be an opportunity to buy some of this amazing traditional craftwork.

K50 FOR A HALF-DAY TOUR

9.00 am	Meet your guides and driver from the local community
10.00 am	Travel to Dorum and explore a traditional village before watching a demonstration of an ancient pottery style by village ladies
11.00 am	A chance to buy some of the amazing pottery and local crafts, bilums and food
12.00 pm	Return to your hotel

Welcome to our paradise!

Our tour is a sustainable community-based tourism project benefiting our village.

Activity 6.3 Design a tour itinerary

Design the itinerary you will give to tourists. Make it accurate, colourful and clearly written in English.

What do tourists want from a tour?

Sustainability

Tourists like to know that their money is going to the local community or a good cause (like a school or church).

Your tour must pay a fair price for access to places, people, traditions and cultures. If this happens it is more likely people will cooperate and be friendly to your guests.

For example, if you bring tourists to see a traditional dance, all the dancers should be paid.

Expert local knowledge

Your guides need to know about the local traditions, stories and history. Tourists always have lots of questions. They might also need the guides to translate for them, so it is essential that the guides speak good English.

Your guides should also be sensible, friendly, calm and confident. They should be respected in the community.

Safety and security

Having a safe tour is very important. You must think of where the risks might be and plan for these. For example:

- transport
- crime
- rivers to cross
- permission to travel to a place
- possible accidents.

Tourists can be nervous about their safety, so plan security carefully.

Professional behaviour

Do not promise something you cannot deliver. Tourists prefer you to be honest about what they will see and do.

If the tourists are overcharged or the tour is not very well organised, word will spread and tourists will stop coming.

Do not drink alcohol, smoke, chew, swear or touch the tourists (apart from shaking hands).

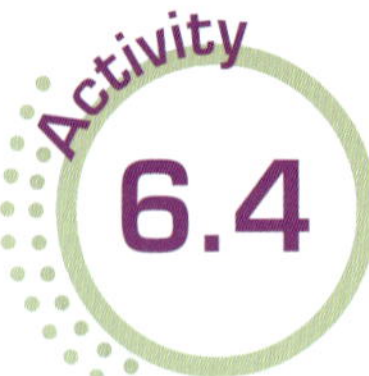

Activity 6.4 Characteristics of a good tour guide

Draw a picture of a male and female tour guide.

- How will they be dressed?
- What expression will be on their faces?
- What will they carry?
- What is their body language?

Now label your tour guides with their characteristics.

For example:

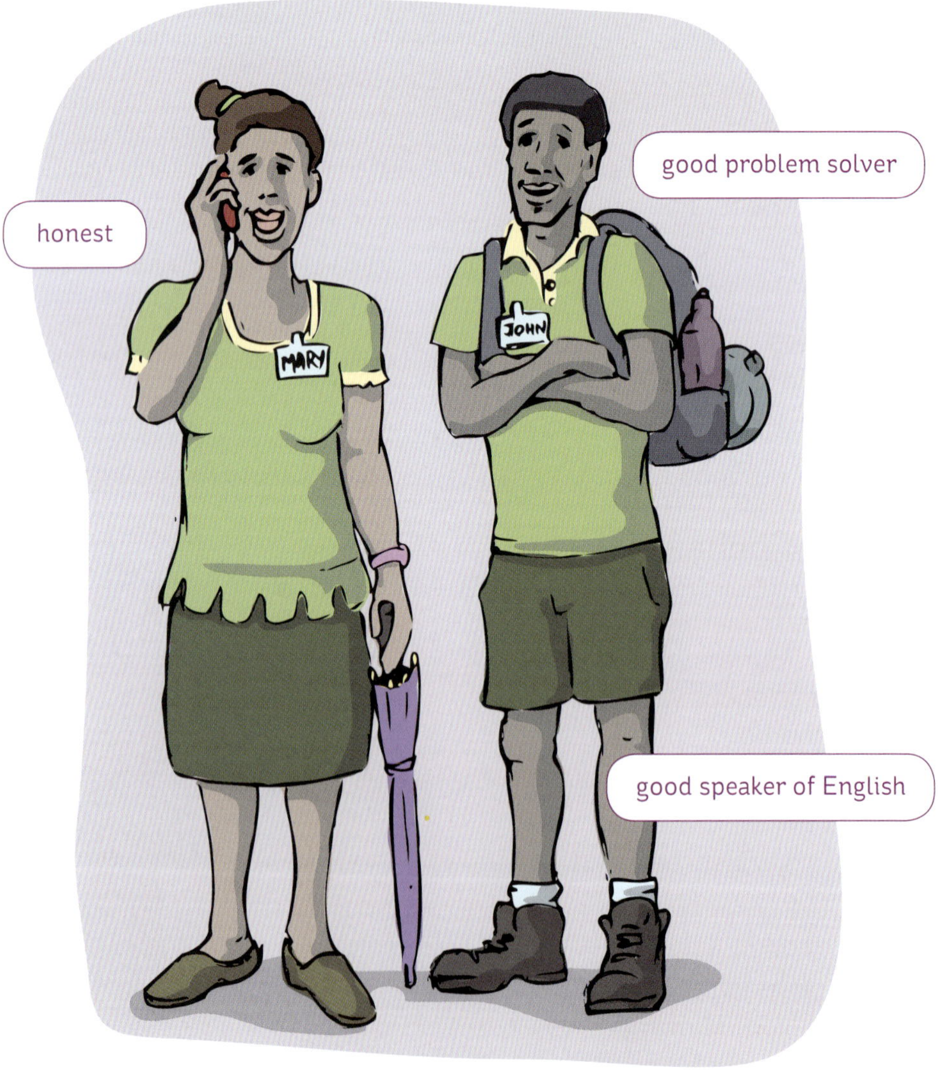

honest
MARY
JOHN
good problem solver
good speaker of English

Chapter 7

Bushwalking and trekking

Adventurous and fit tourists love to explore wilder places. Bushwalking and trekking on trails are very popular activities. Some countries now have professional qualifications for **guides** who escort bushwalkers.

Some tourists want a one-day walk and others will want a longer, multi-day adventure.

In Papua New Guinea there are several well-known and well-organised adventure **treks**:

- Mount Wilhelm, PNG's highest mountain
- Kokoda Track
- Black Cat Trail
- Bulldog Track.

There are different ways of making a living from bushwalking and trekking:

Running a guesthouse on the trekking route

Being a trekking guide

Being a porter or a cook for a trekking group

Being a trekking guide

This work is challenging and you will need special skills, a good attitude and local knowledge to be successful. You will also need to be able to speak good English and have the confidence to lead a group of tourists. Solving problems and making critical decisions is also important. You will need to be fit and healthy.

Keeping your tourists safe is the most important thing you need to remember.

Case study: A mountain guide

Michael is an experienced mountain guide on Mount Wilhelm, PNG's highest mountain.

Tourists can contact him through advertisements he puts up in hotels around PNG. Michael also gets work through recommendations from previous trekkers. His mobile phone is very important.

Michael is a local man who owns land near the mountain. He is able to organise reliable porters and additional guides easily. There are several guesthouses on Mount Wilhelm so Michael also has to work well with them. Maintaining good relationships with the community, landowners and local vehicle drivers is an important part of his work.

Michael speaks excellent English and has warm clothes, waterproofs and tough boots for the mountain climb. He has climbed the mountain many times and knows what to do in an emergency.

To increase his income, Michael and his family welcome guests to their village. Guests can experience a traditional mumu (food cooked in a pit with hot stones) and can explore the traditional Simbu village.

Activity 7.1 Michael the guide

Read the case study about Michael.

1. Which special skills does he have that make him a good trekking guide?
2. What has Michael done to make his small business more successful?
3. If you had any advice to give to Michael about his guiding business, what would it be?
4. What do you think are the most important things a tourist looks for in a trekking guide?

What do tourists look for in a trekking guide?

Safety

Keeping your tourists safe in mountains, forests or remote areas is most important.

You need to know:

- danger points like cliffs and fast rivers
- how to deal with those dangers
- where to go for help and how to arrange a rescue
- basic first aid
- when to turn back (e.g. in bad weather).

Most importantly, you need to know the local area, the trail and the local people well. You will need permission from local people to walk there.

Pace

Setting a safe pace for a trek is very important. Local people might be able to walk all day (10 hours or more) but tourists might struggle.

You need to be able to walk at a pace that does not exhaust your tourists. Spotting when they are too tired or cold will prevent a lot of problems.

Well-equipped and well-planned

You need to have the right gear for your trek to be safe:

- ☑ strong shoes or boots with good grip
- ☑ waterproof coat
- ☑ warm clothes and sleeping bag
- ☑ bush knife
- ☑ pots and pans for cooking
- ☑ torch and spare batteries
- ☑ plastic sheet
- ☑ backpack
- ☑ umbrella or walking stick
- ☑ first aid kit and mosquito net
- ☑ water bottle
- ☑ whistle
- ☑ mobile phone with credit.

Tips

Tourists might not be used to walking in the mountains, especially at high altitude where the air is thinner. If they are out of breath and cannot speak as they walk, slow down the walking pace.

Tips

Female tourists might prefer to have female guides.

Sensible plan and clear instructions

Tourists like to know what is going on, how far they expect to walk and what they will see.

Plan your route and supplies carefully. You might need to send word to local communities to prepare places to stay.

Being able to speak English well is a major advantage.

Getting a good map

You might be able to get a good map from your local mapping office.

In Papua New Guinea the National Mapping Bureau is in Waigani (327 6223).

Your local tourism office could also have maps. You can carefully draw a sketch map for your tourists.

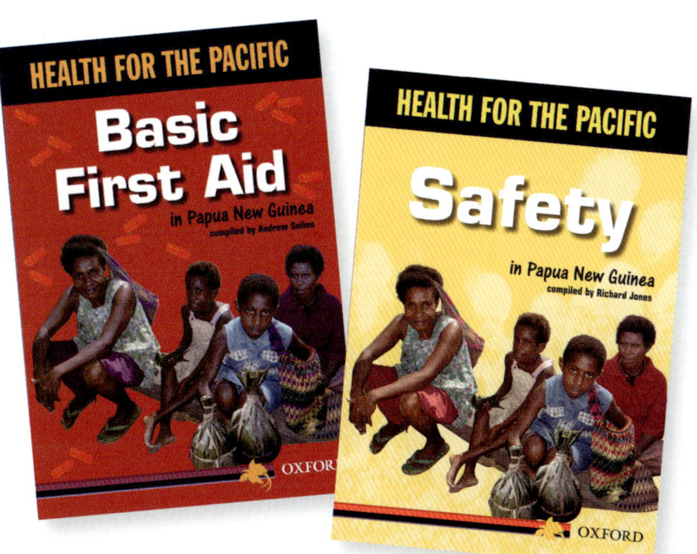

Basic First Aid and *Safety*

These books give more information that could help you and your guests keep safe and healthy.

Activity 7.2 Worst case scenario

You might encounter problems on treks. Discuss these questions for each scenario.

1 What would you do and why?
2 How could this problem have been prevented?

Scenario 1
The trek between two villages normally takes local people about nine hours. After ten hours walking you are still not there and your trekkers are getting very tired and start to complain. It is getting dark.

Scenario 2
Walking down a steep and dangerous path one of your trekkers slips and falls a short distance. They have sprained their ankle and are in a lot of pain.

Scenario 3
Trekking towards the summit of a famous mountain you are surprised by a group of local youths. They block the path and demand money for trespassing on a sacred place.

Scenario 4
As you and your trekkers sit down for their evening meal you hear them complaining about the food (rice and tinned meat).

Scenario 5
You are climbing a high mountain. It is raining and cold. Some of the group are walking faster than others and the slower ones are being left behind.

Scenario 6

You are returning from trekking on a volcano. It starts to rain and the rivers quickly become dangerously deep. There is no other way of crossing and your campsite and supplies are on the other side of the river.

Scenario 7

You are leading a trek in the rainforest. After a couple of nights you feel ill and realise you have malaria. You don't have anyone else to carry the bags.

Scenario 8

You employ several local young men as porters to carry bags. When you arrive at the campsite one of the tourists tells you that some things are missing from their bags.

Now write at least two scenarios for other groups to discuss.

Being a porter

Being a **porter** is a less skilled job than working as a trekking guide.

You will carry the supplies, tents, camping equipment and other materials. Sometimes you will walk ahead of the group and help set up the campsite.

Porters need to be honest and hardworking. They need to be strong. The trekking guide will give you instructions.

In an emergency you might have to help carry injured tourists or take messages to health posts.

Being a cook

Cooking for tourists on a trek is challenging. You need to be able to carry cooking fuel, pots and pans, and all the supplies the group will need.

Ensuring the food is nutritious and the water is safe to drink is a part of your role. Don't forget to wash your hands with soap. Also, some tourists are vegetarians, so make sure you ask before you buy supplies!

Activity 7.3 Buying supplies

You are running a trek for three tourists. They will be walking from village to village for four days and three nights. The path is difficult so they will need plenty of energy. There are no trade stores in the village but you will be able to visit a supermarket in the town first. You have one guide, a cook and two porters.

1. Plan a shopping list and menu for breakfast, snacks, morning tea, lunch, afternoon tea and evening meal. Remember that you have to carry your supplies and you only have two sources of food:
   - store goods
   - vegetables and fruits from the village.
2. List the equipment you will need to cook for your trekking team of seven people (e.g. bowls, plates, cutlery, soap, matches, kerosene, etc.).
3. Work out the budget. How much would you have to charge the tourists?

How much to charge?

Deciding how much money to charge is difficult. Here are a few tips.

- You need one guide for every 2–4 tourists.
- Difficult, long or dangerous treks might have more guides.
- You will need one porter for every 1–2 tourists if you have lots of food and if the tourists are only carrying day packs.
- You might also need to pay for:
  - campsites or community guesthouses
  - food
  - trail fees
  - mobile phone credits
  - a cook.

Plan a trek and advertisement

Plan a trek in your local area. Think about:

- where you will go
- how long it will take
- where your group will stay
- possible dangers and how to deal with them
- food supplies and cooking equipment
- equipment for you and your team
- trail fees and donations you will need to make
- what to pay porters, cooks and other guides
- how much to charge
- a daily itinerary.

Now design an advertisement for tourists which promotes your trek.

Chapter 8

Arts and crafts

Selling arts and crafts to tourists is a popular way of making a living. Tourists are very interested in traditional cultures. You do not need much money to start making baskets, pottery, carvings and woven items. This makes it easier than other activities.

The other main advantage is that the items you make can usually be stored safely until tourists are in your area or can be sold to craft markets or hotels. Making arts and crafts is a good way of preserving traditional skills and knowledge.

What do tourists look for in arts and crafts?

What a tourist decides to buy depends mostly on their personal taste.

Quality

High quality artwork and crafts are much more likely to sell. Tourists will compare different items that local people are selling and will usually notice if yours are not very well made.

Try to use traditional and sustainable materials and make sure you know where they come from if the tourists ask. Avoid using endangered plants, animals and shells, such as turtle shell or bird of paradise feathers.

Fair price

Displaying a fair price on the item is a good idea. You can always negotiate with the tourist if they ask for a lower price.

If people think they have been tricked into spending too much they will be less likely to buy next time.

Customer service

How you speak to tourists is very important.

- Smile, say good day and ask how they are doing.
- Ask if they would like to touch or look at the items.
- Tell them where the items were made, who made them and what they are for. Tourists like to hear the story behind the item.

- Don't put pressure on them – if they like you and your crafts they will buy. If you are too aggressive, they will walk away.
- Think about how you present your items and yourself. Don't smoke, chew or look scruffy. Display your goods carefully.
- Put up a little sign with your name, your home place and a few lines about your work as a craftsperson.
- Have homemade business cards in case a tourist wants a particular design.

Sizes

Think about the kind of tourist you are selling to and what they can carry.

Tourists who are **backpacking** have little space. Tourists on a cruise ship or hotel tour have more space.

Tourists often buy lots of small pieces, which are easy to carry for their friends and family back home. Large pieces are usually for themselves.

Tips

Some traditional crafts might be secret and not to be shared with outsiders. Respect any cultural taboos. Some craft items may have been in your family for a long time and should not be sold.

Your community crafts

Think about your own traditional crafts.

1 Which ones would tourists like to buy?

- **a** What would you say about that craft and its traditional use?
- **b** Could you demonstrate how it would be made?
- **c** Are there any interesting stories about it?

2 How long do they take to make?

3 Where would you sell them?

4 What price would you sell them at to make it worth the effort? Research prices in your local tourist market and hotel shops.

Something different

Be imaginative about your design and making. For example:

- In Papua New Guinea many people make woven bags called bilums. But one clever woman added a zip to her bilums and sold more to tourists.
- Noticing there was a conference at the large resort, one weaver made palm leaf folders for carrying documents and sold many to the business people at the conference.

- A basket weaver realised tourists liked buying sets of baskets, so she planned and made a set in different sizes that fitted together easily for transport.
- Visiting the house of an expat, one local craftsperson realised the traditional fish baskets made beautiful lampshades. He added woven cords and made a slight change to the design of his fish baskets and sold them as lampshades.
- Kava is a traditional drink in many places in the Pacific. One carver decided to make kava coconut shell bowl sets, with carved spoons and a large beautiful bowl. She then put a packet of processed kava in the bowl and sold it as a set to tourists.

Tips

Shell jewellery should only be made with dead shells. Do not kill shells, corals or animals to make crafts. Tourists will want to know you have respected the environment.

Activity 8.2 Thinking about your market

Selling crafts is competitive. There might be hundreds of items for sale in a craft market. Think about what tourists want to buy.

1. How could you change or improve your crafts to improve the chances of it being sold? (Look at the examples above.)
2. How would you make sure your items stood out? (For example, putting them on a small table rather than on the ground.)
3. How could you sell your crafts in more places? (For example, through photographs and adverts in guesthouses and hotels.)
4. Is your item fragile? Could it break easily? How can you package it better for tourists?

Chapter 9 Festivals and cultural shows

There are several ways of making a living from **festivals** and cultural shows.

Taking part in an organised show

There are many large and well-organised cultural shows in Papua New Guinea. Singing and dancing groups can enter these and perform. Sometimes there is a chance you can win prizes or ask for small donations from tourists for photographs.

Famous PNG festivals

National Mask Festival, Kokopo – July
Mount Hagen Show – August
Hiri Moale, Port Moresby – September
Goroka Show – September
Kundu and Canoe Festival, Alotau – November

There are other ways to generate an income at organised shows:

- running a stall selling food
- selling traditional crafts or artwork
- working as a tour guide
- advertising your own tours and community guesthouse to people at the show.

Running a tour to see an arranged traditional dance

In Chapter 6 we looked at different tours. Tourists like to see traditional dances and performances in the village.

These tours can be difficult to arrange because the performers need plenty of time to dress up and do their body paint. You will also need to pay the group.

However, you could offer it as an activity to tourists staying in your community guesthouse and include the chance to wear the costumes and learn a dance.

An example of a popular tour is the visit to the Asaro mudmen in Eastern Highlands Province, Papua New Guinea.

Your local dances and songs

1 Which local dances and songs could be performed for tourists? Remember some might be taboo.

2 Who would be in the dance or song? (e.g. Elementary class.) How many people would perform?

3 Where would they perform?

4 How much time would it take the group to prepare, do the dance and explain the story behind the performance?

5 What would you charge the tourists and how much would you have to contribute to the dancers?

Organising a community festival

Some communities have organised their own traditional festivals or invited tourists to local events. The community we read about in Chapter 1 is one successful example. This is a lot of hard work for the organisers and may not make much money. It does have other benefits such as preserving and promoting traditional culture.

Community involvement and cooperation

It is better to arrange a festival for your own people first and then advertise to tourists later. Festivals which are exciting and important for everyone in the community will be a success whether outsiders come or not.

Without the support of all parts of the community you will not be successful.

You will need an organising committee made up of all the groups in the community:

- men, women, young men and young women, children
- traditional leaders
- councillors
- local school
- churches
- traditional groups
- local businesses (trade stores, mines, hotels, transport, etc.).

Having a theme

Some community festivals have a special theme. This can be as simple as 'Proud of our culture' but it could also be special. It should attract local people, neighbouring villages and international tourists.

For example:

Ambunti Crocodile Festival
Orchid & Flower Festival
Zumim Pottery Show
Kontu & Tembin Shark Calling
Coming-of-age Singsing
Turtle Eco Festival
Yam Festival
Butterfly Festival

Activity

9.2 Deciding a theme for your festival

What name would attract tourists and local people to your festival? What makes your festival unique?

Choosing a date

Choosing a good date for your community festival can make a huge difference. Usually a festival would take a week of preparation, practice and building, so a weekend is a good time to hold a festival. Planning for a public holiday means local tourists are more likely to travel and local school groups could attend.

It is probably best to avoid busy religious festivals unless you can combine the two festivals together. Although tourists travel at Christmas and Easter, the community will be busy.

Make sure your date does not clash with other events in the province. However, you can plan to attract tourists who are visiting larger events and want a village experience.

Remember: the date should be chosen by the community when they want to celebrate their culture.

Think of the whole experience for your international tourists

There is more to a cultural festival than just the traditional dances, costumes and songs. Think about other things a tourist could experience while in your community:

- several different dances and songs with explanations of why they are performed
- night-time storytelling around a fire
- a community guesthouse or home stay
- traditional cooking and gathering of food
- a tour through the local environment
- a visit to the school and church
- the chance to wear a costume and learn a song or dance
- an interview with elders
- a traditional craft sale
- a demonstration of traditional building or craft making.

Plan a community-based festival

Name of the festival: ______________

Community: __________________

Dates: _________________

Who would be on the organising committee?

Which groups will perform?

Which songs and dances will be performed?

Where will these be performed?

What needs to be constructed?

How will we attract neighbouring communities and tourists?

What other activities and tours will we need to arrange for visitors?

How will we make money for the festival? Who will the money go to?

Design an itinerary and advertisement poster for the festival.

Attracting your neighbours

Community-based festivals always attract lots of people from the surrounding villages. To attract as many visitors as possible you should do the following things:

- Advertise the festival well in your area.
- Have a food market and a local crafts market during the festival. Invite neighbouring communities to pay for a small stall.
- Have a litter team to keep the village clean.
- Ban alcohol to prevent fights.
- Organise sporting tournaments (like canoe races) to bring in more people.
- Have cheap local rates for guesthouses and home stays.

- Invite traditional groups to perform in the festival.
- Keep the price for watching the performances low or even free to make sure lots of people come. You will make more money in the market and guesthouses.

Chapter 10

Fishing, snorkelling, canoeing and surfing

Coastal communities can attract tourists by offering fishing, snorkelling, canoeing and surfing activities.

Fishing

The rich seas of the Pacific mean fishing is a simple way to make a living. Some tourists also love to fish and it is a sustainable activity for tourists.

Fishing from a canoe

Fishing from a dinghy

Spear fishing

Fishing from the land

Tourists like to know the environment is being protected, so make sure your community does not fish in a harmful way (for example, by dynamite fishing) and protects its mangroves and reefs.

Demonstrate this by throwing back smaller or rare fish and removing any manmade litter and rubbish from the sea and beach.

Running a fishing trip for a tourist

1 Where are you allowed to fish?
2 Who would be the best canoe or dinghy operator?
3 What equipment would you use and how you would you borrow or loan it?
4 What would you charge for one half-day fishing?
5 Why is it important that a community looks after its reefs, mangroves and beaches?
6 What problems might a fishing trip cause? Why?

Fishing checklist

The following things are necessary before taking tourists fishing:

- ☑ safety equipment such as life jackets
- ☑ fishing equipment
- ☑ knowledgeable fisherman or woman as a guide
- ☑ permission to fish there
- ☑ barbecue or campfire to cook the fish you catch
- ☑ weather, tide and surf check
- ☑ check that the canoe, boat or dinghy is not overloaded
- ☑ water and *kulau* juice
- ☑ sunshade
- ☑ tarpaulin to keep cargo dry.

Snorkelling and swimming

Tourists have all seen amazing pictures of the bright blue sea and clear waters around our islands.

If you live near a pretty beach and good reef, or run a guesthouse nearby, it is a good idea to keep a couple of sets of snorkelling equipment for hire.

Snorkelling and diving are very sustainable activities because tourists do not catch any fish. They just look.

Dive companies using your reefs will usually arrange a small payment to the landowner or community for each diver.

Tips

- Choose a healthy reef about 1–4 metres deep with a colourful mixture of coral and lots of fish.
- Check the currents, tides and surf to make sure it is safe.
- Look out for interesting coral heads and other features like wrecks.
- Keep watch on your snorkellers all the time (from a canoe or the shore).
- Make sure white tourists wear sunscreen and a T-shirt or vest while in the water so they do not get sunburnt.
- A drop of washing-up liquid rubbed into the mask and washed out with water stops the mask from fogging up.
- Make sure you have permission to swim on that reef.
- Tell the tourists not to walk on or touch the living reef.

Coral cuts and stings

If a tourist gets stung or cut you should treat it immediately with vinegar or hot water.

Coral cuts can get infected, so the tourist should cover the cut with a plaster and use antibiotic cream.

Canoeing

Learning how to use a traditional canoe is an experience tourists will not forget.

You can organise simple canoe trips to places of interest, such as special reefs, wrecks or river mouths.

Remind the tourists that they should be strong swimmers, wear a hat and T-shirt, and bring some water. Paddling can be hard work!

Beaches

Tourists love having a swim and a picnic on a beautiful tropical beach.

Tips

- Keep the beach clean of manmade rubbish and any animal waste.
- Give tourists a warm welcome and explain where they can and cannot walk and swim.
- Provide a barbecue place.
- Give the tourists privacy, peace and quiet.
- If you want to charge a small fee, make sure you display the price clearly.

What tourists wear ...

Some tourists like to get a suntan. They might wear a bikini or short shorts on your community's beach.

1. Would this be acceptable in your culture? Why or why not?
2. What can you do to prevent tourists causing offence?
3. Role-play how to tell a female tourist not to wear a bikini while walking around your village.

Surfing

Surfers travel from all over the world to surf on surf breaks. If you have regular, large waves near your community for some months of the year, surfers might be interested in visiting.

Inviting local and international surfers to explore your area is one way to find out if people will want to surf there.

Surfing is a sustainable activity because it does not damage the environment. Surf culture is about adventure and exploration and if you make surfers welcome they will continue to visit your beaches.

Tips

If your community has a good surf break and surfers are visiting, here are some ways you can make a living:

- Send text messages to local surfers when the breaks look good.
- Build a bush material surf lodge on the beach.
- Build a community guesthouse.
- Sell cool drinks, food and snacks to the surfers.
- Watch their cars and equipment.
- Set up a washing place.
- Collect a regular and fair surf management fee for each surfer.
- Ask your surf association for donated surfboards.

Diving

Diving is very popular with tourists and dive operations are careful not to damage reefs. Running a dive resort or dive boat needs a special set of skills and costs a lot of money for training, insurance and the diving equipment. However, it is still possible for small tourist projects to make some money from divers.

Site fees

If your community owns a reef or wreck where divers like to dive, you should be able to negotiate a site fee.

This could be an annual payment from the dive company or a small fee for each diver for each dive. Sometimes this will be made to a clan or community fund.

If you charge a site fee you will be expected to protect the dive site from over-fishing and other damage to the reef. You will also be responsible for looking after the mooring for the dive boats.

Selling to dive boats

Large dive boats are at sea for many days and visit many dive sites.

Communities can sometimes sell fresh fruits, vegetables and fish to the dive boat.

You can also arrange for divers to come ashore to buy traditional arts and crafts.

Last day activities

Divers cannot dive for 24 hours before they fly home so this is a time when they like to relax and explore the local culture.

Tours, cultural songs and dances and other small tourist activities would be popular with divers.

Discuss what you can offer divers with your local dive companies and resorts.

Advantages and disadvantages

1 What are the advantages and disadvantages of allowing beach and sea activities in your local area?

2 What problems might you face in setting up a tourism activity like fishing or surfing?

3 How could you overcome these problems?

Chapter 11 Ecotourism and sustainability

Ecotourism is when you run a tourism activity which does not harm the environment. Sometimes it might even help the environment. Ecotourism also promotes local, community-based tourism which benefits local people.

Tourists want to feel their activities do not harm the environment or local cultures. The tourism should be ethical.

Activity 11.1 Ecotourism code of conduct

Leave nothing but footprints
Take nothing but photographs and memories
Kill nothing but time
Don't leave anything behind you except a good impression

1 Discuss this well-known code for ecotourism with a friend. What does each part mean?

2 Give an example of a tourism activity for each quote.

3 Can you add any other ecotourism rules for protecting the environment and traditional cultures?

What might an ecotourism activity look like?

Using nature sustainably

- using food from gardens
- building guesthouses from bush materials
- asking tourists not to waste food or water
- building toilets in a healthy place
- not using rare plants or animals in food, traditional crafts or costumes
- using solar and hydro power
- walking, canoeing, cycling and swimming.

Dealing with waste

- picking up litter
- not throwing manmade rubbish in the sea, street or bush
- burning or burying manmade waste properly.

Protecting sensitive areas

- banning logging and hunting in certain areas
- agreeing to a 'no-fishing' area on the reef
- not cutting mangroves
- not fishing with dynamite.

Not disturbing rare animals and birds

- leaving nests and eggs alone
- moving quietly through the forest
- throwing back small or rare fish.

Educating

- talking about what you are doing and why
- educating tourists about how your community protects the environment
- valuing and promoting your culture and traditional way of life.

Activity 11.2 Your community

1 Choose one of the tourism activities you have planned in this book and list how you will make it eco-friendly and reduce the impact on the environment and culture.

2 Write a letter to the tourist who asked this question:

Chapter

12 Finances

Keeping your finances organised is important. You should take into account the amount of money you will need to start your project and what you will need to charge to make a **profit**.

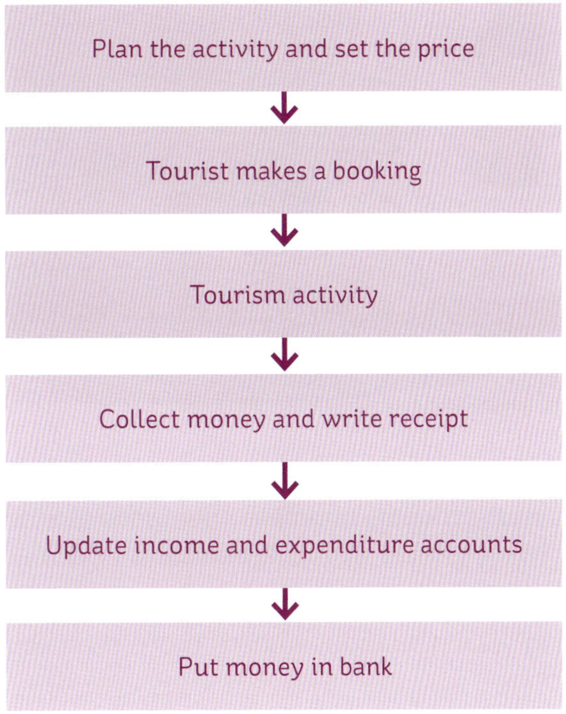

At a minimum you need to have:

- a price list
- a bookings register
- a receipt book
- an account book with income and expenditure columns.

Some other useful things to help with managing the finances are:

- a mobile phone
- homemade business cards
- advertisements and flyers
- a bank account or microfinance account
- a trusted friend to check your figures and books
- a loan repayment book if you need a microfinance loan to get started.

Setting the price

One of the most difficult things about running a small tourism project is making a profit. It is easy to underestimate the costs of starting up and running the activity. Many people also overestimate how many visitors they will get or baskets they will sell.

If building and running your guesthouse costs more than you get from visitors you will have lost money.

Profit and loss

For each of these tourism activities calculate whether the person will be making a profit.

a Did they make a profit or loss?

b How could they improve their profits? Give some suggestions.

c What would happen if they had more guests? What if they had fewer guests?

1

EXPENDITURE

Building the guest house:

K250 for sheets, pots, pans, plates, cups, cutlery
K100 for kerosene stove
K80 for kerosene lamps
K200 for nails and tools for building the guesthouse (bush material)

Running the guesthouse:

K30 Photocopying adverts and buying a guestbook
K240 Store food from trade store
K40 Market food
K60 Fuel
K30 Mobile phone credit

INCOME (2010)

Accommodation:

K100 2 × tourist, 1 night @ K50/head
K150 1 × tourist, 3 nights @K50/head
K50 1 × tourist, 1 night @K50/head
K200 4 × local Government workers, 2 nights, K25/head

Meals:

K280 Evening meals × 14 @ K20/head
K140 Breakfast × 14 @K10/head

2

Eddie's Waterfall Tour

EXPENDITURE

Guide equipment:

K10 Umbrella
K30 Backpack
K50 Mobile phone

Running the tour:

K50 Transport costs to bus company
K100 Landowners of waterfall
K20 Porter
K10 Mobile phone credit

INCOME (2010)

K250 5 × tourists, half-day tour @K50/head

Getting start-up money

You might need a little money to start your tourism project. For larger projects like village festivals and building a guesthouse you will need the support of your family or clan.

There are several sources for start-up money:

- your own savings
- a loan from your family
- a microfinance loan
- a bank loan.

A bank loan will be hard to get if you do not have a job and a money lender might charge you too much interest which you will not be able to pay back.

Activity 12.2 Ranking

1 Rank this list of activities from cheapest to most expensive start-up costs.

Guesthouse	Surf lodge	Pottery making
Basket weaving	Canoe trips	Tours
Snorkelling	Fishing	Dancing at festivals
Running a local festival	Market stall	Trekking

2 List the best people and organisations for micro-credit loans in your area. What are the lending rules?

Remember: start small and invest your profits back into the business.

For example:

Start out as a porter on a trekking route.
Save the money and buy better trekking clothes, boots, mobile phone.
Print business cards and advertisements.

Work as a guide.
Save the money and buy materials for a guesthouse.

Build a guesthouse for trekkers.
Save money.
Start to run tours and hire your own guides.

↓

Buy a vehicle for transporting trekkers and local people.
Save money.

Activity 12.3 Goal setting

What are your goals for your business?

Profit at the end of year 1: ______________

Number of tourists/items sold: ______________

My goal for my business in five years' time is: ______________

Chapter 13 Working well with your community

Successful tourism projects work closely with the local community. Being able to communicate and cooperate with your family and community will help you make a living.

You will need to explain why you think the business is a good idea and how it will respect the local culture and environment.

This is a common fear and sometimes people will be jealous of your success. Thinking of ways to share the profits through the community will help. However, the business is also for you to make a living.

Large resorts have a much bigger impact on the environment and on the community.

You should be able to say why people might come and visit. Explain your advertising and what numbers you are expecting.

Case study 1: Guesthouse problems

Community A built a guesthouse several years ago by a pretty beach and barbecue area. It was popular with local tourists and a few international ones. However, basic maintenance was not done and the building began to look more and more rundown. Sheets were not replaced and the fly wire was broken. Eventually no more visitors came.

Case study 2: Angry community

Mr B had set up a little business showing tourists to the summit of a nearby volcano. He led them through gardens and villages on the climb to the summit. Community leaders asked him if he was making payments to the landowners and he said he was, but he wasn't. Once local men found out, they chased the tourists away.

Case study 3: Bilum makers

Mr C bought bilums from local women for a few kina and then sold them at the local tourist market. One day, a woman from the community noticed Mr C was charging the tourists a lot more than he was paying them. He had lied to them about how much he earned. She told the others and they stopped selling to him.

Case study 4: Stealing

Miss D was running a successful guesthouse and she had many visitors. Most local people were pleased and supportive. However, drunken young men from her family started causing problems, especially when there were lone white females staying. One night someone broke in and stole the guests' bags. Miss D had to close the guesthouse.

Case study 5: Taboo

Mr and Mrs E ran tours from their community guesthouse. One day their tour guide took a group of men to the women's traditional washing place. This was a secret place and led to arguments in the village. The tourists were very embarrassed.

Activity 13.1 Discussion

1 What lessons can you learn from these case studies?
2 List reasons why some tourism projects fail.
3 Which of these reasons are the most common? Why are they common problems?
4 How could these problems be prevented?

Tips for working well with the community

- Keep them informed regularly.
- Ask them for advice and help.
- Think of ways of sharing the work and profits.
- Respect their culture and environment.
- Anticipate what problems might happen and plan solutions.
- Find out how people have done this in the past.
- Be a responsible role model and behave well.

Chapter 14 Working well with the tourism industry

Local hotels and resorts

Many tourists who visit large hotels and resorts will want to experience community-based tourism and village life.

Most hotels and resorts want to support local tourism projects. They do this in a number of ways:

- putting up advertisements
- making recommendations
- including your advertisements and price list in information folders in their guest rooms
- hiring local tour guides
- buying crafts and artwork for sale in their shop
- training local people in tourism.

Case study: Support from a hotel or resort

This PNG hotel has been supporting local community-based tourism for many years. The town is popular with divers and backpackers because of its good reefs and safe environment. There are also lots of conferences in the town.

The hotel has worked hard to encourage community-based tourism. A network of community guesthouses and tours has been established. The hotel promotes these local projects and helps communities improve customer care and the visitors' experiences.

The hotel's guest information pack includes information on tours and visits to nearby communities. Many tourists who stay in the hotel in town also travel out to stay in the local guesthouses and take part in tours run by villagers.

Research

Visit resorts and hotels in your local area. Ask to see their guestbook and interview a senior member of staff.

1 How does the hotel support community-based tourism?

2 How does the hotel decide which projects to promote or support?

3 Which local tourism projects does the hotel support?

Other community-based tourism projects

You can work in partnership with other projects. For example:

- organising treks to another community's guesthouse
- sharing information, lessons and contacts
- advertising your tours in their guesthouse
- helping out in Making a Living lessons at the primary school
- going to guesthouses in other communities to sell crafts to their guests
- training other communities in tourism.

Your local tourism office

It is essential you work with your local tourism office. They can advertise your project and let you know of any special events coming up.

- Keep your posters and leaflets up to date.
- If you change your phone number let them know quickly.
- Ask to be put on their website.
- Regularly visit and update them on your activities and numbers of tourists.

International advertising

There are guidebooks for international tourists that can be very useful. It is worth reading one.

One of the most popular is the Lonely Planet guidebooks. They often list grassroots tourism projects and guesthouses.

Tourists will often post comments about great places they visited, stayed in, and tours they did on the Lonely Planet website. They also record bad experiences!

Chapter 15 Customer care

Almost all your visitors will be interested in and respectful of your community. They will be curious about how you live and your culture.

However, you might sometimes run into problems and it is better to be prepared.

Why are some tourists difficult customers?

They are stressed by heat, tiredness, strange culture, hunger.

They are not sensitive about local culture.

They don't understand what is going on.

They think they are being cheated.

Their expectations are not being met.

They are scared or nervous.

Preventing problems with guests

- Anticipate problems before they happen:
  - have clear written prices
  - have simple guesthouse rules
  - provide an itinerary
  - explain what will happen and when it might happen
  - keep in contact by mobile phone or text message.
- Ask them regularly if they are okay and happy.
- Listen to the tourists and watch their expressions.
- Stay calm and smile.
- Make sure you understand what the problem is.
- Be honest and try and deal with the problem quickly.
- Find someone who speaks their language to help communicate well.

Activity 15.1 Role play

Work with a peer to role-play successful solutions to these problems. Practice calm body language and assertive speaking. Be polite.

1 Taboos

2 Complaints

3 Value for money

4 Language problems

5 Alcohol

Now prepare at least two more scenarios when you might have to deal with a difficult tourist; for example, dealing with a late pick-up.

Local tourists

As our country becomes richer more local people will travel as tourists. Perhaps they might come and visit relatives or they want to experience a part of the country they have not seen before. Many will come on business or with the public sector.

Local tourists might not have as much money, so you may have to change your prices. They are very likely to take gifts and practical crafts back with them.

Getting feedback

Feedback helps you improve your business. You should regularly ask your tourists about their visit or their purchase. Some people give a simple feedback form but you can just ask them.

For example:

How did you enjoy the food?

POOR GREAT

How could we improve the food?

____

____

____

Design a feedback form or questionnaire

1 Design a feedback form for one of the following businesses:

- **a** a community guesthouse
- **b** a tour.

- What questions would you ask?
- What rating systems would you use?
- Can you fit it into no more than one side of paper? It must be quick to fill out.

2 If you are able, compare your form to one from a large hotel or resort.

Chapter 16 Getting started

Making a living for you and your family is a big challenge but very rewarding. Community-based tourism is part of developing a community and promotes self-reliance. It is also more likely to be eco-friendly and respectful of local cultures.

Tourism is a sustainable way of helping people experience your unique culture and environment. With life skills, hard work, problem solving and persistence you can earn a living from tourism.

Using the tips and checklists in this book will help. We wish you success with your tourism project.

Activity 16.1 Timeline

Plan a timeline for implementing a tourism project which would work in your community.

- What are the main steps?
- Who do you need to consult at each stage?
- When can the first income start?
- When will you start making a profit?
- What will happen in one, two and five years' time?

16.2 Comparing tourism activities

With a group of peers, compare the tourism activities in the book.

Activity	Advantages	Disadvantages	How easy is it to make a profit? 1=easy, 5=hard
Community guesthouse			
Tour guide			
Trekking guide			
Trekking porter			
Making and selling crafts			
Organising a festival			
Taking part in a large festival			
Fishing trips			
Snorkelling trips			
Canoe trips			
Home stay			
Birdwatching			

Activity

16.3 Action planning

Reflect on what you have learnt. Plan for a tourism activity.

My project is ______________________________

It will be based in ______________________________

First of all, I will ______________________________

Then, I will ______________________________

I will need to learn how to ______________________________

I will need help from ______________________________

I will get my start-up money from ______________________________

I think that by the end of the year ______________________________

I aim to make ______________ by the end of ______________

I will work with my family and community in these ways:

____

I will advertise by ______________________________

I will improve my project by ______________________________

If you need more information about tourism

Visiting your local tourism office is an excellent starting point. You can also contact the Tourism Promotion Authority in Port Moresby:

PNG Tourism Promotion Authority
PO Box 1291
Port Moresby
NCD
Ph: 3200211
Fax: 3200223
Email: info@pngtourism.org.pg

Many tourism offices have websites that give information about tourism services in the Pacific:

Papua New Guinea	www.pngtourism.org.pg
Vanuatu	www.vanuatu.travel
Solomon Islands	www.visitsolomons.com.sb
Fiji	www.fijime.com
Tonga	www.tongaholiday.com
Samoa	www.samoa.travel

www.lonelyplanet.com is a popular guidebook series.

You could also contact these organisations for information:

Surf Association of Papua New Guinea
www.surfingpapuanewguinea.org.pg
Ph: 320 0211

Dive Association of Papua New Guinea
www.pngdive.com
PO Box 1646
Port Moresby
NCD

Glossary

backpackers	tourists who are travelling on a tight budget and without much cargo
community-based tourism	small-scale locally run tourism activities
ecotourism	tourism activities that try not to damage the environment
entrepreneur	a person who sets up a new business
festival	a cultural event with traditional dancing, music and activities
guide	a person who leads a group of tourists on a trek or tour
home stay	when a tourist stays in your home and experiences life with your family
host	a person in charge of a guesthouse or home stay
international tourist	a tourist from another country
itinerary	a plan of activities for tourists
local tourist	a tourist who travels to another part of his or her own country
market research	finding out what your customers want
porter	a person who carries cargo on a trek
profit	money left after you have paid your expenses
surf breaks	a large wave which breaks in a way surfers can ride
sustainable	an activity which does not remove resources from a community
tour	when tourists are escorted to a place or event of interest
tourist	a person visiting another place for interest and pleasure
trek	an adventurous walk in a remote place. Can be more than one day.
vegetarian	a person who does not eat meat

Acknowledgments

The author and the publisher wish to thank the following copyright holders for reproduction of their material.

Photos: iStockphoto/ Jodi Jacobson, p. 58; Katrina Heydon, p. 54; Richard Jones, front cover top left, front cover centre left, pp. 2, 9, 11 top & bottom, 12, 24, 27 top & bottom, 43 top left, 43 right, 43 bottom left, 44, 45, 47 top, 52, 53 top & bottom, 56, 57, 59, 61, 64 top left & right, 64 bottom right, 67 top & bottom, 68, 71, 73, 84, 86 top, 91, 93; Lonely Planet, reproduced with permission from Lonely Planet Papua New Guinea 8th Edition © 2008 Lonely Planet, p. 86 bottom; Jennifer Miller, front cover bottom left & right, pp. 30, 36, 39, 60 top & bottom; Photolibrary/ Ron Dahlquist, p. 64 bottom left/ François Gilson, p. 72; Shutterstock/ Capturefoto, p. 6/ Brian Chase, p. 66/ Sebastien Burel, p. 69.

Every effort has been made to trace the original source of copyright material contained in this book. The publisher will be pleased to hear from copyright holders to rectify any errors or omissions.

Notes

Notes